PAINLESS

SPANISH

CONVERSATION

1

1ST EDITION
FEBRUARY, 2020

SARA TYLER

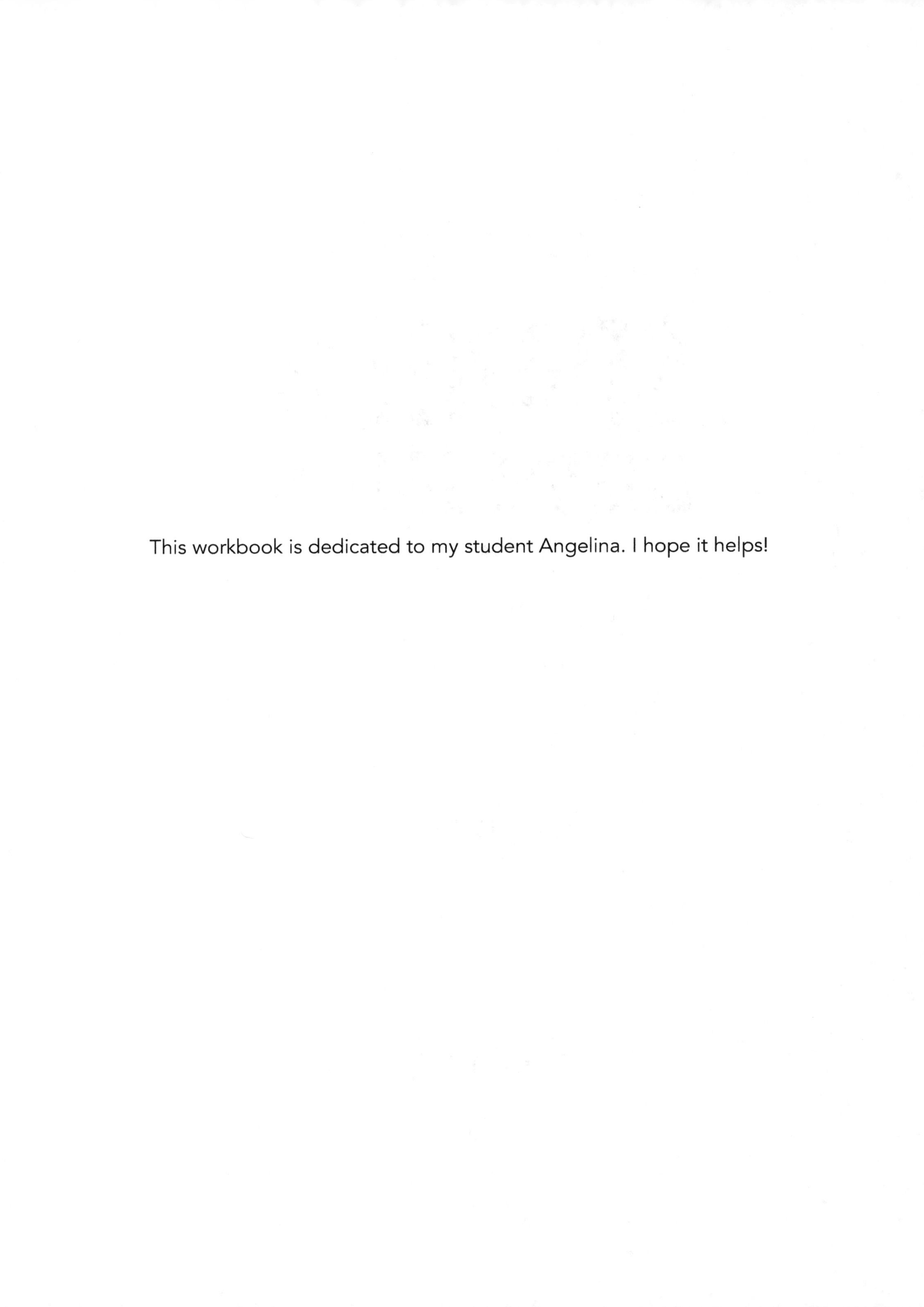

This workbook is dedicated to my student Angelina. I hope it helps!

ABOUT THIS BOOK

Thank you for your interest in my workbook. This has been a project that I wanted to begin for a long time. I've been teaching for 10 years now. Just in the past year, I've had over 500 Spanish students in online classes.

Overwhelmingly, what students want is conversation practice. The majority of the students that have taken classes with me aren't learning it for academic credit. They want to travel abroad, have better professional opportunities, or communicate with loved ones who are Spanish speakers.

The strategy in this workbook is what I use in live classes. It has been extremely successful for students of all ages. In addition, it's how my husband improves his English. Since his needs are for immediate communication within the house, with myself and our daughters.

I start by introducing the yo form only with regular verbs. Students only have to remember the -o ending (Traditional workbooks teach 12 new pronouns and 6 endings for every verb). Then, we add in the tú form, with two more endings, so that we can ask and answer questions. By doing this, students speak right away. They are also practicing to most used forms of the verb, (yo and tú), which is more practical for their goals.

This is why you will find common verbs and vocabulary that can be used in everyday life, around the house, or in the car. Students who are able to practice the vocabulary on a daily basis are more likely to retain it, as well as continue to study Spanish.

Sara Tyler
teachersaratyler@gmail.com

WORKBOOK SET-UP

Here you will find the tense, grammar structure, verb form and interrogative word that you should use.

Each page has the verb endings you will need.

-ER verb ending

PRETERITE / QUESTIONS / TÚ / CUÁNDO   verb endings: **-aste / -iste**

-AR verb ending

SPANISH	ENGLISH	QUESTION	VERB/SUBJECT	OBJECT
cenar	to eat dinner	¿Cuándo	cenaste	pizza?
comer	to eat			
tomar	to drink			
estudiar	to study			
trabajar	to work			
cocinar	to cook			
limpiar	to clean			
escribir	to write			
ayudar	to help			
manejar	to drive			
leer	to read			
preparar	to prepare			
necesitar	to need			
lavar	to wash			
llevar	to bring			
usar	to use/wear			
mirar	to watch			
comprar	to buy			
cuidar	to care for			
arreglar	to fix			
guardar	to put away			

Columns help you realize if you are missing a part of the grammar structure.

Shaded verbs must have objects.

TABLE OF CONTENTS

VERB CONJUGATION / PRESENT TENSE

In Spanish, the verb changes each time the subject (a person doing an action) does. The changes to the end of the verb are called **verb conjugation**.

For English speakers, We rely on pronouns to tell us who is doing the action. As a result, learning the conjugations to all of the verb forms is overwhelming and frustrating.

This is why you will practice verb conjugation starting in the **yo** (I) form first. Then, you will learn the tú form (you). With these two forms, you will be able to ask and answer questions, and communicate on a variety of topics.

Remember, in Spanish, the verb's ending tells us who the subject is. So often times, subject pronouns are not used. You will have to rely on the verb to tell you who and what is happening.

SPANISH	ENGLISH	VERB/SUBJECT	OBJECT
hablar	to speak	Hablo	español.

In order to conjugate a regular verb, you first remove the last two letters (-**AR, -ER** or -**IR**).

If the verb is hablar, as seen above, you end up with the root **habl**-.

Then, you add the new ending to the verb. The yo form always ends in o. So, **hablo** means I speak. When you begin to make questions, you will use -as endings for verbs that end in -**AR** and -es for those that end in -**ER** or -**IR**.

PRESENT / AFFIRMATIVE / NEGATIVE / YO verb endings: **-o**

*For negative statements, put **no** before the verb. Example: **No** ceno.

SPANISH	ENGLISH	AFFIRMATIVE	NEGATIVE
cenar	to eat dinner	Ceno.	No ceno.
comer	to eat		
tomar	to drink		
estudiar	to study		
trabajar	to work		
cocinar	to cook		
limpiar	to clean		
escribir	to write		
ayudar	to help		
manejar	to drive		
leer	to read		
preparar	to prepare		
necesitar	to need		
lavar	to wash		
llevar	to bring		
usar	to use/wear		
mirar	to watch		
comprar	to buy		
cuidar	to care for		
arreglar	to fix		
guardar	to put away		

FORMING DETAILED QUESTIONS AND ANSWERS

Not all verbs require an object. But, objects can make your questions and answers more specific and interesting. You will also need them to answer specific questions, like the ones we will practice in this workbook. Objects can be anything that receives the action of the verb.

In addition to objects another way to make your questions and answers more specific and detailed is to add prepositional phrases a time or place.

You will find both objects and prepositional phrases throughout the workbook to help you. There are additional vocabulary lists at the end if the section.

All of these options mean that there are many ways to answer the same question, and still be correct.

With the present tense, we will focus on using the following question words:

SPANISH	ENGLISH	ANSWERS CAN INCLUDE
(de/con) qué	(of/with) what	a noun (person, place or thing)
cuándo	when	a time (exact time, time period, day, month, etc.
a qué hora	at what time	an exact time
dónde	where	a place (room, building, area, city, county, etc.)
con quién	with whom	a person (name, other descriptive words like doctor, father, woman, friend, etc.)

There are even more regular verbs, objects and expressions that you can use. But this workbook is meant to give students the most common verbs, and repetition, that they need to communicate in Spanish right away.

SPANISH	ENGLISH
COMIDA	**FOOD**
la leche	milk
el agua	water
el café	coffee
el refresco	soda
la fruta	fruits
los vegetales	vegetables
el brócoli	broccoli
la lechuga	lettuce
la cebolla	onion
el tomate	tomato
el pepino	cucumber
el pimiento	pepper
el plátano	banana
la manzana	apple
la naranja	orange
la piña	pineapple
la fresa	strawberry
las uvas	grapes
el pollo	chicken
el res	beef
el cerdo	pork
el jamón	ham
el queso	cheese
el cereal	cereal
las galletas	cookies
las galletas saladas	crackers
el yogur	yogurt

PRESENT / QUESTIONS / TÚ / QUÉ

verb endings: **-as** / **-es**

SPANISH	ENGLISH	QUESTION	VERB/SUBJECT
cenar	to eat dinner	¿Qué	cenas?
comer	to eat		
tomar	to drink		
estudiar	to study		
trabajar	to work	¿De qué	
cocinar	to cook		
limpiar	to clean		
escribir	to write		
ayudar	to help	¿Con qué	
manejar	to drive		
leer	to read		
preparar	to prepare		
necesitar	to need		
lavar	to wash		
llevar	to bring		
usar	to use/wear		
mirar	to watch		
comprar	to buy		
cuidar	to care for		
arreglar	to fix		
guardar	to put away		

verb endings: **-o**

SPANISH	ENGLISH	VERB/SUBJECT	OBJECT
cenar	to eat dinner	Ceno	pizza.
comer	to eat		
tomar	to drink		
estudiar	to study		
trabajar	to work		
cocinar	to cook		
limpiar	to clean		
escribir	to write		
ayudar	to help		
manejar	to drive		
leer	to read		
preparar	to prepare		
necesitar	to need		
lavar	to wash		
llevar	to bring		
usar	to use/wear		
mirar	to watch		
comprar	to buy		
cuidar	to care for		
arreglar	to fix		
guardar	to put away		

*The word **do** isn't needed in Spanish to make negative sentences or questions.

SPANISH	ENGLISH	VERB/SUBJECT	OBJECT
cenar	to eat dinner	¿Cenas	pizza?
comer	to eat		
tomar	to drink		
estudiar	to study		
trabajar	to work		
cocinar	to cook		
limpiar	to clean		
escribir	to write		
ayudar	to help		
manejar	to drive		
leer	to read		
preparar	to prepare		
necesitar	to need		
lavar	to wash		
llevar	to bring		
usar	to use/wear		
mirar	to watch		
comprar	to buy		
cuidar	to care for		
arreglar	to fix		
guardar	to put away		

verb endings: **-o**

SPANISH	ENGLISH	SÍ / NO	VERB/SUBJECT + OBJECT (optional)
cenar	to eat dinner	Sí.	Ceno pizza.
comer	to eat		
tomar	to drink		
estudiar	to study		
trabajar	to work		
cocinar	to cook		
limpiar	to clean		
escribir	to write		
ayudar	to help		
manejar	to drive		
leer	to read		
preparar	to prepare		
necesitar	to need		
lavar	to wash		
llevar	to bring		
usar	to use/wear		
mirar	to watch		
comprar	to buy		
cuidar	to care for		
arreglar	to fix		
guardar	to put away		

VOCABULARY

SPANISH	ENGLISH
TIEMPO	**TIME**
en la mañana	in the morning
en la tarde	in the afternoon
en la noche	in the evening
el lunes	Monday
el martes	Tuesday
el miércoles	Wednesday
el jueves	Thursday
el viernes	Friday
el sábado	Saturday
el domingo	Sunday
el fin de la semana	weekend
entre la semana	during the week
todo el día	all day
siempre	always
con frecuencia	frequently
a veces	sometimes
de vez en cuando	once in a while
nunca	never

*For exact times, use **a las** in front of the hour (**a las 7**). Use **a la** in front of 1 (**a la 1**).

Use **el + day of the week to say on Monday, Tuesday, etc.
Use **los + day of the week** to say every Monday / on Mondays, etc.

verb endings: **-as** / **-es**

SPANISH	ENGLISH	QUESTION	VERB/SUBJECT
cenar	to eat dinner	¿Cuándo	cenas?
comer	to eat		
tomar	to drink		
estudiar	to study		
trabajar	to work		
cocinar	to cook		
limpiar	to clean		
escribir	to write		
ayudar	to help		
manejar	to drive		
leer	to read		
preparar	to prepare		
necesitar	to need		
lavar	to wash		
llevar	to bring		
usar	to use/wear		
mirar	to watch		
comprar	to buy		
cuidar	to care for		
arreglar	to fix		
guardar	to put away		

verb endings: **-o**

*Possible time expressions: days, months, frecuency

SPANISH	ENGLISH	VERB/SUBJECT	TIME
cenar	to eat dinner	Ceno	a las 8 y 30.
comer	to eat		
tomar	to drink		
estudiar	to study		
trabajar	to work		
cocinar	to cook		
limpiar	to clean		
escribir	to write		
ayudar	to help		
manejar	to drive		
leer	to read		
preparar	to prepare		
necesitar	to need		
lavar	to wash		
llevar	to bring		
usar	to use/wear		
mirar	to watch		
comprar	to buy		
cuidar	to care for		
arreglar	to fix		
guardar	to put away		

SPANISH	ENGLISH	QUESTION	VERB/SUBJECT	OBJECT
cenar	to eat dinner	¿Cuándo	cenas	pizza?
comer	to eat			
tomar	to drink			
estudiar	to study			
trabajar	to work			
cocinar	to cook			
limpiar	to clean			
escribir	to write			
ayudar	to help			
manejar	to drive			
leer	to read			
preparar	to prepare			
necesitar	to need			
lavar	to wash			
llevar	to bring			
usar	to use/wear			
mirar	to watch			
comprar	to buy			
cuidar	to care for			
arreglar	to fix			
guardar	to put away			

SPANISH	ENGLISH	VERB/SUBJECT	TIME
cenar	to eat dinner	Ceno pizza	los viernes.
comer	to eat		
tomar	to drink		
estudiar	to study		
trabajar	to work		
cocinar	to cook		
limpiar	to clean		
escribir	to write		
ayudar	to help		
manejar	to drive		
leer	to read		
preparar	to prepare		
necesitar	to need		
lavar	to wash		
llevar	to bring		
usar	to use/wear		
mirar	to watch		
comprar	to buy		
cuidar	to care for		
arreglar	to fix		
guardar	to put away		

SPANISH	ENGLISH
LA CASA	**HOME**
la sala	living room
el comedor	dining room
la cocina	kitchen
el dormitorio	bedroom
el baño	bathroom
el ático	attic
el sótano	basement
la ventana	window
la puerta	door
el techo	wall
la pared	roof
el piso	floor
el cerámico	ceramic
la madera	wood
el concreto	concrete
el vidrio	glass
el patio	patio
el jardín	backyard
la terraza	deck
la piscina	swimming pool
la ducha	shower
la bañera	bath
la taza	toilet
el lavabo	sink
el closet	closet
el mostrador	counter
el gabinete	cabinet

SPANISH	ENGLISH	QUESTION	VERB/SUBJECT + OBJECT
cenar	to eat dinner	¿Dónde	cenas?
comer	to eat		
tomar	to drink		
estudiar	to study		
trabajar	to work		
cocinar	to cook		
limpiar	to clean		
escribir	to write		
ayudar	to help		
manejar	to drive		
leer	to read		
preparar	to prepare		
necesitar	to need		
lavar	to wash		
llevar	to bring		
usar	to use/wear		
mirar	to watch		
comprar	to buy		
cuidar	to care for		
arreglar	to fix		
guardar	to put away		

SPANISH	ENGLISH	POSITIVE	NEGATIVE
cenar	to eat dinner	Ceno en el comedor.	No ceno.
comer	to eat		
tomar	to drink		
estudiar	to study		
trabajar	to work		
cocinar	to cook		
limpiar	to clean		
escribir	to write		
ayudar	to help		
manejar	to drive		
leer	to read		
preparar	to prepare		
necesitar	to need		
lavar	to wash		
llevar	to bring		
usar	to use/wear		
mirar	to watch		
comprar	to buy		
cuidar	to care for		
arreglar	to fix		
guardar	to put away		

SPANISH	ENGLISH	VERB/SUBJECT + OBJECT	PLACE
cenar	to eat dinner	Ceno pizza	en la cocina.
comer	to eat		
tomar	to drink		
estudiar	to study		
trabajar	to work		
cocinar	to cook		
limpiar	to clean		
escribir	to write		
ayudar	to help		
manejar	to drive		
leer	to read		
preparar	to prepare		
necesitar	to need		
lavar	to wash		
llevar	to bring		
usar	to use/wear		
mirar	to watch		
comprar	to buy		
cuidar	to care for		
arreglar	to fix		
guardar	to put away		

SPANISH	ENGLISH	SPANISH	ENGLISH
LA FAMILIA	**FAMILY**	**GENTE**	**PEOPLE**
la madre	mother	el bebé	baby
el padre	father	el niño	boy
el hermano	brother	la niña	girl
la hermana	sister	el adolescente	teenager
la abuela	grandmother	la mujer	woman
el abuelo	grandfather	el hombre	man
la tía	aunt	el amigo/a	friend
el tío	uncle	la novia	girlfriend
la prima	cousin	el novio	boyfriend
el hijo	son	la pareja	couple
la hija	daughter	la novia	bride
el sobrino	nephew	el novio	groom
la sobrina	niece	el vendedor/a	salesperson
la madrastra	stepmother	el cajero/a	cashier
el padrastro	stepfather	el doctor/a	doctor
el hermanastro	stepbrother	el enfermero/a	nurse
la hermanastra	stepsister	el policia	police officer
el medio hermano	half-brother	el profesor/a	teacher
la media hermana	half-sister	el director/a	principal
la madre / el padre biológico/a	biological mother/father	el estudiante	student
la madre / el padre adoptivo/a	adoptive mother/father	el guardia	security guard
el hijo adoptado	adopted son	el niñero/a	babysitter
la hija adoptada	adopted daughter		
la madrina	godmother		
el padrino	godfather		

TIPS

*When the direct object is a person, an **a** is put directly before it (Cuido **a** mi hija.).

    verb endings: **-as** / **-es**

SPANISH	ENGLISH	QUESTION	VERB/SUBJECT + OBJECT
cenar	to eat dinner	¿Con quién	cenas?
comer	to eat		
tomar	to drink		
estudiar	to study		
trabajar	to work		
cocinar	to cook		
limpiar	to clean		
escribir	to write		
ayudar	to help		
manejar	to drive		
leer	to read		
preparar	to prepare		
necesitar	to need		
lavar	to wash		
llevar	to bring		
usar	to use/wear		
mirar	to watch		
comprar	to buy		
cuidar	to care for		
arreglar	to fix		
guardar	to put away		

SPANISH	ENGLISH	VERB/SUBJECT	OBJECT	PLACE
cenar	to eat dinner	Ceno	pizza	con mi mamá.
comer	to eat			
tomar	to drink			
estudiar	to study			
trabajar	to work			
cocinar	to cook			
limpiar	to clean			
escribir	to write			
ayudar	to help			
manejar	to drive			
leer	to read			
preparar	to prepare			
necesitar	to need			
lavar	to wash			
llevar	to bring			
usar	to use/wear			
mirar	to watch			
comprar	to buy			
cuidar	to care for			
arreglar	to fix			
guardar	to put away			

VERB CONJUGATION / PRETERITE TENSE

Now that you've had practice with the present tense, we're going to start working on the **preterite** tense. The preterite is the same as the simple past in English. It is used for one time actions that are finished.

Since it's very important for the actions in the past to have an exact time, you will hear more time expressions in this tense.

The simple past is also more definite than the present tense. You won't be able to use habitual expressions like sometimes or always.

Look at the new endings for -AR verbs in the first example, and -ER / -IR in the second.

SPANISH	ENGLISH
Habl**é** español.	I spoke Spanish.
¿Habl**aste** español?	Did you speak Spanish?

Com**í** sushi.	I ate sushi.
¿Com**iste** sushi?	Did you eat sushi?

SPANISH	ENGLISH	AFFIRMATIVE	NEGATIVE
cenar	to eat dinner	Cené.	No cené.
comer	to eat		
tomar	to drink		
estudiar	to study		
trabajar	to work		
cocinar	to cook		
limpiar	to clean		
escribir	to write		
ayudar	to help		
manejar	to drive		
leer	to read		
preparar	to prepare		
necesitar	to need		
lavar	to wash		
llevar	to bring		
usar	to use/wear		
mirar	to watch		
comprar	to buy		
cuidar	to care for		
arreglar	to fix		
guardar	to put away		

SPANISH	ENGLISH	SPANISH	ENGLISH
EN LA CASA	**IN THE HOUSE**	**ELECTRÓNICOS ELECTRODOMÉSTICOS**	**ELECTRONICS APPLIANCES**
el sofá	sofa	la lavadora	washing machine
el sillón	armchair	el refrigerador	fridge
la mesa del centro	coffee table	la estufa	stove
la mesita	end table	el horno	oven
el estante	stand / shelf	el televisión	TV
la planta	plant	el teléfono	phone
la cama	bed	el celular	cellphone
la almohada	pillow	la tableta	tablet
la cobija	cover	la computadora	computer
la cuna	crib	la laptop	laptop
las literas	bunk beds	la aspiradora	vacuum
el escritorio	desk	el proyector	projector
el ropero	dresser	la cafetera	coffee maker
la mesa	table	la licuadora	blender
la silla	chair	el microondas	microwave
el plato	plate	el congelador	freezer
el plato hondo	bowl	la bocina	speaker
la taza	cup	los audífonos	earbuds
la servilleta	napkin	el aire acondicionado	air conditioning
el sartén	frying pan		
la olla	pot	el ventilador	fan
la espátula	spatula	el router	router
el tenedor	fork	el internet / in línea	internet
la cuchara	spoon	la nube	cloud
el cuchillo	knife	el WiFi	WiFi

verb endings: **-aste /-iste**

SPANISH	ENGLISH	VERB/SUBJECT	OBJECT
cenar	to eat dinner	¿Cenaste	pizza?
comer	to eat		
tomar	to drink		
estudiar	to study		
trabajar	to work		
cocinar	to cook		
limpiar	to clean		
escribir	to write		
ayudar	to help		
manejar	to drive		
leer	to read		
preparar	to prepare		
necesitar	to need		
lavar	to wash		
llevar	to bring		
usar	to use/wear		
mirar	to watch		
comprar	to buy		
cuidar	to care for		
arreglar	to fix		
guardar	to put away		

SPANISH	ENGLISH	SÍ / NO	VERB/SUBJECT + OBJECT (optional)
cenar	to eat dinner	Sí.	Cené pizza.
comer	to eat		
tomar	to drink		
estudiar	to study		
trabajar	to work		
cocinar	to cook		
limpiar	to clean		
escribir	to write		
ayudar	to help		
manejar	to drive		
leer	to read		
preparar	to prepare		
necesitar	to need		
lavar	to wash		
llevar	to bring		
usar	to use/wear		
mirar	to watch		
comprar	to buy		
cuidar	to care for		
arreglar	to fix		
guardar	to put away		

SPANISH	ENGLISH	QUESTION	VERB/SUBJECT
cenar	to eat dinner	¿Qué	cenaste?
comer	to eat		
tomar	to drink		
estudiar	to study		
trabajar	to work	¿De qué	
cocinar	to cook		
limpiar	to clean		
escribir	to write		
ayudar	to help	¿Con qué	
manejar	to drive		
leer	to read		
preparar	to prepare		
necesitar	to need		
lavar	to wash		
llevar	to bring		
usar	to use/wear		
mirar	to watch		
comprar	to buy		
cuidar	to care for		
arreglar	to fix		
guardar	to put away		

verb endings: **-é** / **-í**

SPANISH	ENGLISH	VERB/SUBJECT	OBJECT
cenar	to eat dinner	Cené	pizza.
comer	to eat		
tomar	to drink		
estudiar	to study		
trabajar	to work		
cocinar	to cook		
limpiar	to clean		
escribir	to write		
ayudar	to help		
manejar	to drive		
leer	to read		
preparar	to prepare		
necesitar	to need		
lavar	to wash		
llevar	to bring		
usar	to use/wear		
mirar	to watch		
comprar	to buy		
cuidar	to care for		
arreglar	to fix		
guardar	to put away		

VOCABULARY

SPANISH	ENGLISH
TIEMPO	**TIME**
en la mañana	in the morning
en la tarde	in the afternoon
en la noche	in the evening
el lunes pasado	last Monday
la semana pasada	last week
el fin de la semana pasado	last weekend
el mes pasado	last month
el año pasado	last year
hoy	today
ayer	yesterday
anteayer	the day before yesterday
anoche	last night
el 14 de febrero	February 14th
en 2018	In 2018
en mayo	In May
hace una hora	1 hour ago
hace un día	1 day ago
hace 2 semanas	2 weeks ago
hace mucho tiempo	a long time ago

SPANISH	ENGLISH	QUESTION	VERB/SUBJECT
cenar	to eat dinner	¿Cuándo	cenaste?
comer	to eat		
tomar	to drink		
estudiar	to study		
trabajar	to work		
cocinar	to cook		
limpiar	to clean		
escribir	to write		
ayudar	to help		
manejar	to drive		
leer	to read		
preparar	to prepare		
necesitar	to need		
lavar	to wash		
llevar	to bring		
usar	to use/wear		
mirar	to watch		
comprar	to buy		
cuidar	to care for		
arreglar	to fix		
guardar	to put away		

verb endings: **-é / í**

SPANISH	ENGLISH	VERB/SUBJECT	TIME
cenar	to eat dinner	Cené	a las 8 y 30.
comer	to eat		
tomar	to drink		
estudiar	to study		
trabajar	to work		
cocinar	to cook		
limpiar	to clean		
escribir	to write		
ayudar	to help		
manejar	to drive		
leer	to read		
preparar	to prepare		
necesitar	to need		
lavar	to wash		
llevar	to bring		
usar	to use/wear		
mirar	to watch		
comprar	to buy		
cuidar	to care for		
arreglar	to fix		
guardar	to put away		

PRETERITE / QUESTIONS / TÚ / CUÁNDO   verb endings: **-aste** / **-iste**

SPANISH	ENGLISH	QUESTION	VERB/SUBJECT	OBJECT
cenar	to eat dinner	¿Cuándo	cenaste	pizza?
comer	to eat			
tomar	to drink			
estudiar	to study			
trabajar	to work			
cocinar	to cook			
limpiar	to clean			
escribir	to write			
ayudar	to help			
manejar	to drive			
leer	to read			
preparar	to prepare			
necesitar	to need			
lavar	to wash			
llevar	to bring			
usar	to use/wear			
mirar	to watch			
comprar	to buy			
cuidar	to care for			
arreglar	to fix			
guardar	to put away			

verb endings: **-é / í**

SPANISH	ENGLISH	VERB/SUBJECT	TIME
cenar	to eat dinner	Cené pizza	el viernes pasado.
comer	to eat		
tomar	to drink		
estudiar	to study		
trabajar	to work		
cocinar	to cook		
limpiar	to clean		
escribir	to write		
ayudar	to help		
manejar	to drive		
leer	to read		
preparar	to prepare		
necesitar	to need		
lavar	to wash		
llevar	to bring		
usar	to use/wear		
mirar	to watch		
comprar	to buy		
cuidar	to care for		
arreglar	to fix		
guardar	to put away		

PRETERITE / QUESTIONS / TÚ / DÓNDE   verb endings: **-aste** / **-iste**

SPANISH	ENGLISH	QUESTION	VERB/SUBJECT + OBJECT
cenar	to eat dinner	¿Dónde	cenaste?
comer	to eat		
tomar	to drink		
estudiar	to study		
trabajar	to work		
cocinar	to cook		
limpiar	to clean		
escribir	to write		
ayudar	to help		
manejar	to drive		
leer	to read		
preparar	to prepare		
necesitar	to need		
lavar	to wash		
llevar	to bring		
usar	to use/wear		
mirar	to watch		
comprar	to buy		
cuidar	to care for		
arreglar	to fix		
guardar	to put away		

SPANISH	ENGLISH	POSITIVE	NEGATIVE
cenar	to eat dinner	Cené en el comedor.	No cené.
comer	to eat		
tomar	to drink		
estudiar	to study		
trabajar	to work		
cocinar	to cook		
limpiar	to clean		
escribir	to write		
ayudar	to help		
manejar	to drive		
leer	to read		
preparar	to prepare		
necesitar	to need		
lavar	to wash		
llevar	to bring		
usar	to use/wear		
mirar	to watch		
comprar	to buy		
cuidar	to care for		
arreglar	to fix		
guardar	to put away		

SPANISH	ENGLISH
LUGARES	**PLACES**
el hospital	hospital
la escuela	school
la casa	home
la farmacia	pharmacy
el supermercado	supermarket
la playa	beach
el aeropuerto	airport
la gasolinera	gas station
el parque	park
el mercado	market
el cine	movie theatre
el carro	car
el avión	airplane
el autobús	bus
la bicicleta	bicycle

verb endings: **-é / í**

SPANISH	ENGLISH	VERB/SUBJECT + OBJECT	PLACE
cenar	to eat dinner	Cené pizza	en la cocina.
comer	to eat		
tomar	to drink		
estudiar	to study		
trabajar	to work		
cocinar	to cook		
limpiar	to clean		
escribir	to write		
ayudar	to help		
manejar	to drive		
leer	to read		
preparar	to prepare		
necesitar	to need		
lavar	to wash		
llevar	to bring		
usar	to use/wear		
mirar	to watch		
comprar	to buy		
cuidar	to care for		
arreglar	to fix		
guardar	to put away		

SPANISH	ENGLISH	SPANISH	ENGLISH
LA FAMILIA	**FAMILY**	**GENTE**	**PEOPLE**
la madre	mother	el bebé	baby
el padre	father	el niño	boy
el hermano	brother	la niña	girl
la hermana	sister	el adolescente	teenager
la abuela	grandmother	la mujer	woman
el abuelo	grandfather	el hombre	man
la tía	aunt	el amigo/a	friend
el tío	uncle	la novia	girlfriend
la prima	cousin	el novio	boyfriend
el hijo	son	la pareja	couple
la hija	daughter	la novia	bride
el sobrino	nephew	el novio	groom
la sobrina	niece	el vendedor/a	salesperson
la madrastra	stepmother	el cajero/a	cashier
el padrastro	stepfather	el doctor/a	doctor
el hermanastro	stepbrother	el enfermero/a	nurse
la hermanastra	stepsister	el policia	police officer
el medio hermano	half-brother	el profesor/a	teacher
la media hermana	half-sister	el director/a	principal
la madre / el padre biológico/a	biological mother/father	el estudiante	student
la madre / el padre adoptivo/a	adoptive mother/father	el guardia	security guard
el hijo adoptado	adopted son	el niñero/a	babysitter
la hija adoptada	adopted daughter		
la madrina	godmother		
el padrino	godfather		

TIPS

*When the direct object is a person, an **a** is put directly before it (Cuido **a** mi hija.).

SPANISH	ENGLISH	QUESTION	VERB/SUBJECT + OBJECT
cenar	to eat dinner	¿Con quién	cenaste?
comer	to eat		
tomar	to drink		
estudiar	to study		
trabajar	to work		
cocinar	to cook		
limpiar	to clean		
escribir	to write		
ayudar	to help		
manejar	to drive		
leer	to read		
preparar	to prepare		
necesitar	to need		
lavar	to wash		
llevar	to bring		
usar	to use/wear		
mirar	to watch		
comprar	to buy		
cuidar	to care for		
arreglar	to fix		
guardar	to put away		

verb endings: **-é / í**

SPANISH	ENGLISH	VERB/SUBJECT	OBJECT	PLACE
cenar	to eat dinner	Cené	pizza	con mi mamá.
comer	to eat			
tomar	to drink			
estudiar	to study			
trabajar	to work			
cocinar	to cook			
limpiar	to clean			
escribir	to write			
ayudar	to help			
manejar	to drive			
leer	to read			
preparar	to prepare			
necesitar	to need			
lavar	to wash			
llevar	to bring			
usar	to use/wear			
mirar	to watch			
comprar	to buy			
cuidar	to care for			
arreglar	to fix			
guardar	to put away			